Halloween Alphabet

Halloween Alphabet

Beverly Barras Vidrine
Illustrated by Alison Davis Lyne

PELICAN PUBLISHING COMPANY
Gretna 2004

For Jeanie and Pete
—B. B. V.

For my parents
—A. D. L.

*The word "Pelican" and the depiction of a pelican are trademarks
of Pelican Publishing Company, Inc., and are registered
in the U.S. Patent and Trademark Office.*

Library of Congress Cataloging-in-Publication Data

Vidrine, Beverly Barras.
  Halloween alphabet / by Beverly Barras Vidrine ; illustrated by Alison Davis Lyne.
    p. cm.
  Summary: Explores Halloween traditions represented by each letter of the alphabet, from the old game of bobbing for apples to a Zorro costume.
  ISBN 1-58980-242-X (pbk. : alk. paper)
  1. Halloween—Juvenile literature. [1. Halloween. 2. Alphabet.] I. Lyne, Alison Davis, ill. II. Title.

  GT4965.V53 2004
  394.2646—dc22

2004003452

"Z"™ and the character of "Zorro"® are used with the express permission of Zorro Productions, Inc., Berkeley, CA © 2003. All Rights Reserved.

Printed in Singapore

Published by Pelican Publishing Company, Inc.
1000 Burmaster Street, Gretna, Louisiana 70053

HALLOWEEN ALPHABET

Years ago, the Celtic (KEL tik) people celebrated the harvest of fruits and vegetables. Many of these foods were orange. About the same time, they had a festival for the dead called Samhain (SAH ween). The Celts believed the spirits of dead people came back to haunt them in the black of the night. Today's fall celebrations and the Halloween colors of black and orange go back to these old traditions and superstitions.

A is for apple. One, two, or more apples float in a tub of water. Bobbing for them is an old game that is still played with this delicious fruit.

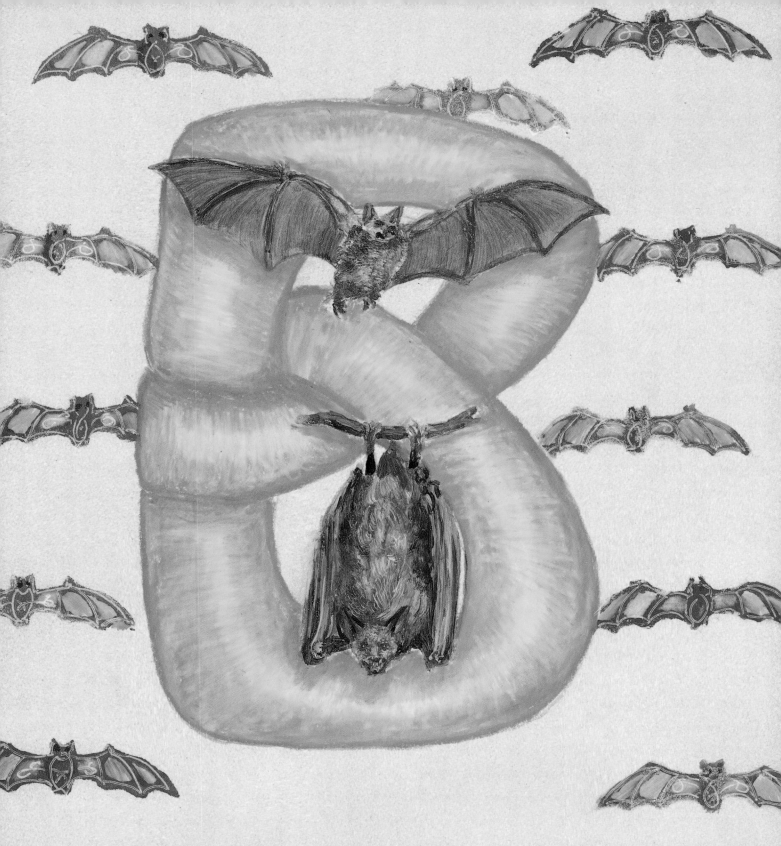

B is for bat. Most bats hang down, rolled up, and sleep in caves or trees with other bats. This creature of the night really scared people of long ago.

C is for cat. The favorite pet animal of the witch creeps around by the light of the moon. It's just a superstition that black cats bring bad luck.

D is for dummy. The harvest dummy is made from clothes stuffed with straw. At one time, it was placed next to a house to protect the family from winter storms.

E is for eve. It's the evening before All Hallows' Day or All Saints' Day. With time, All Hallows' Eve changed to Halloween, but the date is still October 31.

F is for fear. In times past, grownups and children were afraid of the long and dark winter nights. They worried and imagined witches flying and ghosts floating.

G is for ghost and goblin. Old folk tales tell how these evil spirits appeared on Halloween. They were supposed to haunt places and spook everyone.

H is for haunted house. An old, empty house may be set up with dancing ghosts. Bells ring and scary music plays to thrill children as they walk through the dark rooms.

I is for Irish. These settlers brought some Halloween customs to America:

bobbing for apples, carving jack-o'-lanterns, and going trick-or-treating.

J is for jack-o'-lantern. The name comes from an old Irish story about Jack. He walked the roads at night carrying a hollow turnip lighted by a candle. People called him "Jack of the Lantern."

K is for kettle. A cauldron (KAWL drun), or kettle, boils the witch's brew. Some tales say that the old hag cooked plants and spices to make magic potions.

L is for lollipop. Candy makers shape hard candy on a stick into pumpkins and ghosts. Children fill their bags with suckers, candy corn, sweets, and other treats.

M is for mask. Long ago, the Celts wore animal heads and dressed in animal skins. They hoped the ghosts would not recognize them. Now masks are worn just for fun.

N is for Nutcrack Night. This celebration took place long ago on October 31. People enjoyed the good harvest of nuts by eating them and using some to play fortune-telling games.

O is for owl. The bird with big eyes swoops down and
hoots. Many people once believed that witches turned
into owls.

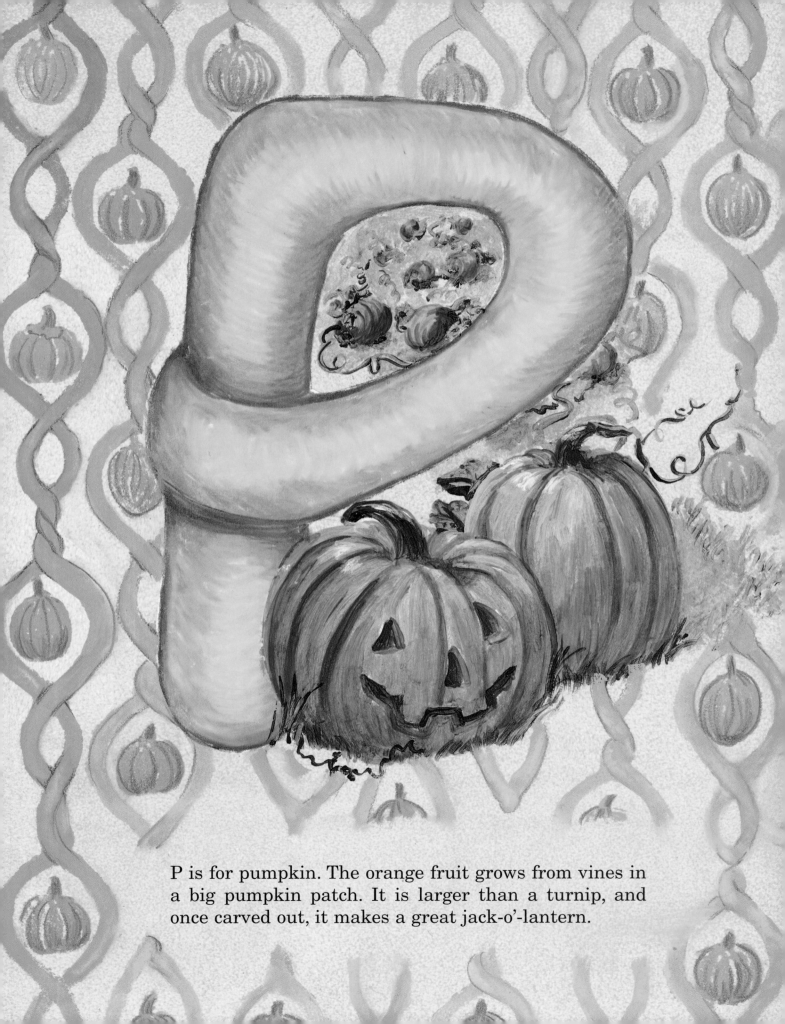

P is for pumpkin. The orange fruit grows from vines in a big pumpkin patch. It is larger than a turnip, and once carved out, it makes a great jack-o'-lantern.

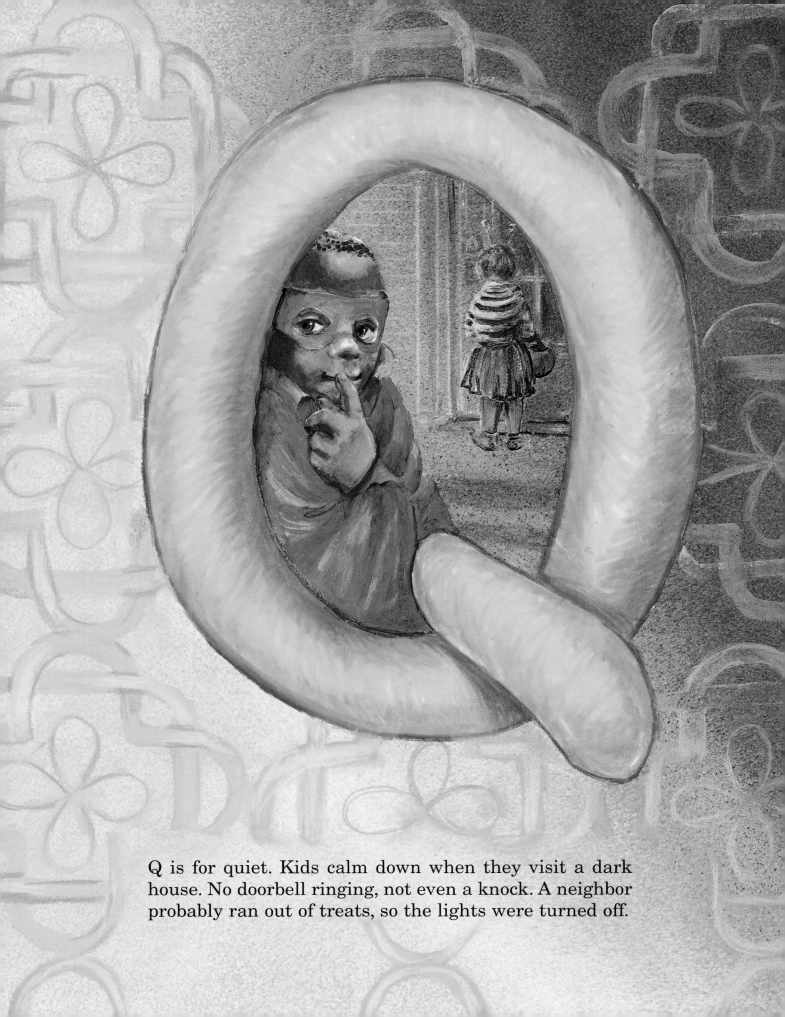

Q is for quiet. Kids calm down when they visit a dark house. No doorbell ringing, not even a knock. A neighbor probably ran out of treats, so the lights were turned off.

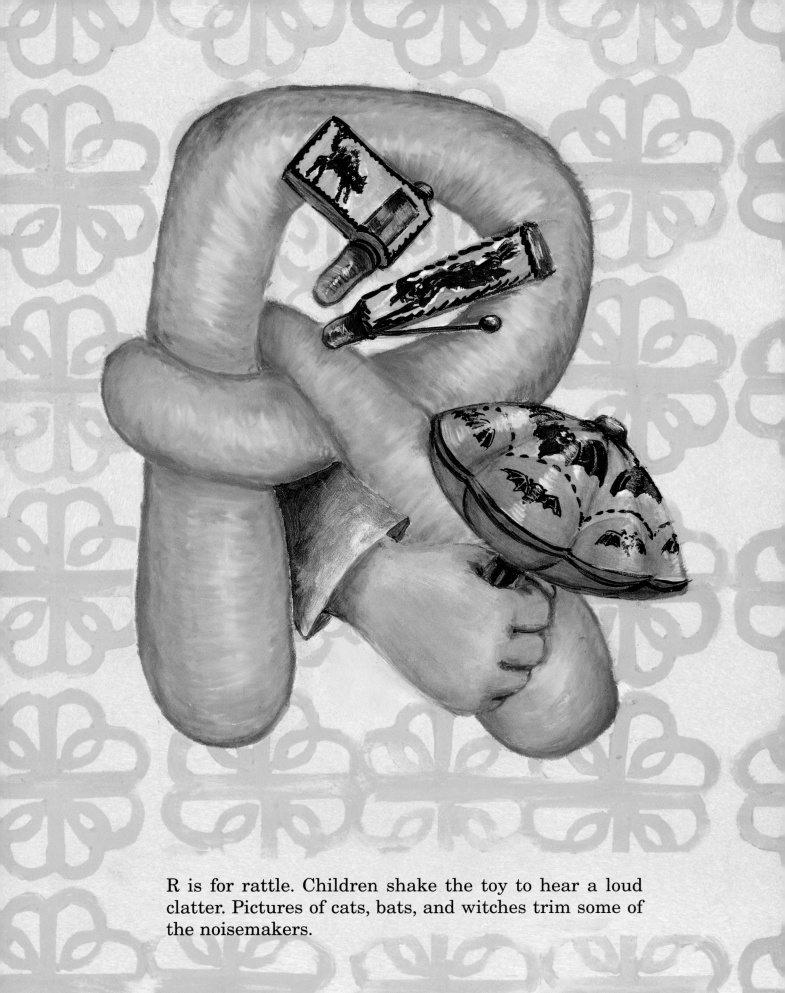

R is for rattle. Children shake the toy to hear a loud clatter. Pictures of cats, bats, and witches trim some of the noisemakers.

S is for saint and soul. On November 1, All Saints' Day, Catholic churches honor holy people who have died. On November 2, All Souls' Day, Christians pray for their dead relatives and friends.

T is for "trick or treat." The Halloween cry is yelled by children who want sweets to eat. In Irish stories, farmers went from house to house begging for food. If they didn't get any, they played a prank, like hiding a cow.

U is for ugly. Sometimes an awful face is carved out of a pumpkin. People of long ago believed that a horrible jack-o'-lantern kept the witches and ghosts away.

V is for vampire. The creature from folk tales wears a cape to look like a bat. Now vampire costumes are popular because of these stories.

W is for witch. In the old days, a witch was known as a wise woman who had magic powers. People thought she wore black at night so no one could see her riding on a broomstick.

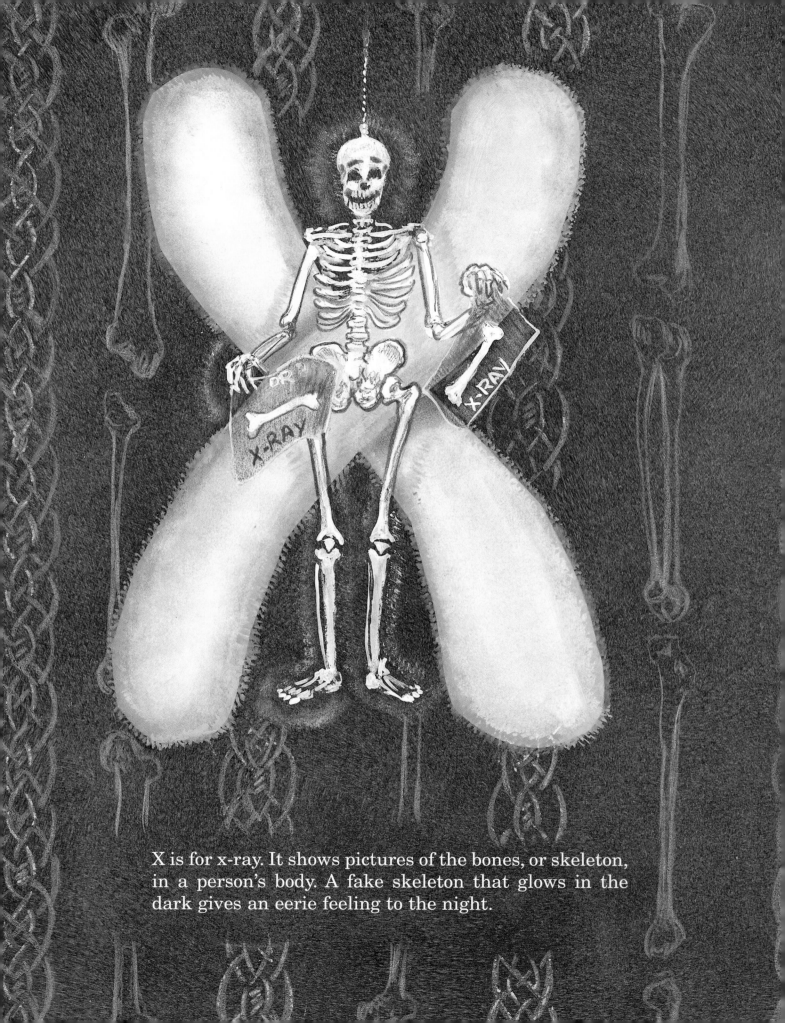

X is for x-ray. It shows pictures of the bones, or skeleton, in a person's body. A fake skeleton that glows in the dark gives an eerie feeling to the night.

Y is for yard. Some scary front lawns look like make-believe graveyards. Ghosts, tombstones, and monsters decorate the grounds.

Z is for Zorro®. Zorro® dresses in black, with a mask and a cape. He fights for justice. Zorro® leaves his mark, the letter Z™, where he has been.